TRANQUIL SEAS

Books by Nora D'Ecclesis...

Mastering Tranquility
A Guide to Developing Powerful Stress Management Skills

Tranquil Seas
Applying Guided Visualization

Reiki Roundtable

TRANQUIL SEAS

Applying Guided Visualization

Nora D'Ecclesis

Copyright © 2013 by Nora D'Ecclesis

All rights reserved. No part of this book may be reproduced by any mechanical, photographic, or electronic processes, or in the form of an audio recording; nor may it be stored in a retrieval system, transmitted, or otherwise copied for public or private use without written permission of the author.

The material in this book is for informational purposes only. As each individual situation is unique, you should use proper discretion, in consultation with a health care practitioner, before undertaking any exercise, recipe, technique or practice described in this book. The author and publisher are not responsible in any manner whatsoever for any injury that may occur through following the instructions in this material. The activities, physical and otherwise, described herein for informational purposes, may be too strenuous for some people and the reader should consult a physician before engaging in them.

Published by Renaissance Presentations, King of Prussia, PA
ISBN-13: 978-0615881195
ISBN-10: 061588119X
First Edition: March 2013
Printed in the United States of America

Dedicated to:

My husband, Dr. David, who was born in the Colorado Rocky Mountains and raised near the magnificent Pacific Ocean in California.

I married him at 19 and he has taught me everything I know about the great outdoors! No woman could ask for a more supportive life companion.

My expectation is for many more days together out on the lake where he still puts the worm on my hook.

Table of Contents

FOREWORD..ix
PREFACE...xi
INTRODUCTION – PREVENTING STRESS.......................................1
MIND: MASTERING TRANQUILITY THROUGH GUIDED VISUALIZATIONS.......5
MIRROR NEURONS AND GUIDED VISUALIZATION...........................9
STRENGTH OF THE MIND...19
RESTORATION...25
KEEP IN MIND...33
QUICK START GUIDE TO MEDITATIVE VISUALIZATION....................35

GUIDED VISUALIZATIONS

THE MAGNIFICENCE OF THE MAGNOLIA TREE IN BLOOM.................39
THE PESSE CANOE GLIDES...43
DOWN THE JERSEY SHORE...47
THE MAJESTIC VIEW OF THE SNOW-CAPPED MOUNTAIN..................51
SNOWING LIKE A RUSSIAN NOVEL..57
VIBRATIONAL LEVEL UP AFTER THE END OF A RELATIONSHIP...........63
PRINCIPLES OF THE MASTER..67
TRANQUIL SEAS RETREAT...73
ELEVATE THOUGHTS AS I CLIMB TOWARD THE HEAVENS................79
RUNNING AS MEDITATION...85

ILLUSTRATIVE JOURNALS

    SHAWN ACOSTA..93
    DIANA BROWN..103
    HEATHER IMIELINSKI...107
    CINDY SNOW..109

ONE MINUTE RESPITE..113
PARTING THOUGHTS...115
APPENDIX..117

Foreword

Nora has had decades of training in her field and like a high intensity laser-beam she can cut instantly to the core of any issue. And her answer usually is one of tranquility. To seek the stillness that lies within all of us, if only we would let the seas of turmoil calm, and then in that moment of calmness we learn the answers, which in fact are quite simple...But it takes someone with wisdom to see that clearly and help guide you to it.

That is her gift. That is the purpose I see in her life. She is a guide to tranquility and in that tranquility, answers that were there all along, visible just below the surface once the waters have become still and there just below the surface are the truths she can point you towards. I thank God she is and always will be part of my life.

It has been one of the great pleasures of my life to be able to say that Nora D'Ecclesis was the first friend of my life (we were neighbors and born but a few months apart) and has stood by my side in good times and in tough times as the decades unfolded. Perhaps not a coincidence that so many years ago she was one of the first to encourage me to pursue a career in writing and in turn I always felt her remarkable talents needed to be shared with a far wider audience than those whom she interacts directly with through her counseling, retreats and workshops. Thus it is a pure delight for me to be able to recommend this her second work, building on the wonderful success of her first publication of several years ago. You will find in the good doctor's writing sage advice, guidance and a warm heart that will quickly touch into yours and provide perspective, a perspective I have always turned to without hesitation when needed. So many years ago, Nora could trump any childhood argument with "I am four months older than you," thus ending most debates with that wisdom and logic of childhood. I have come to learn that Nora is indeed older, older in a spiritual sense with a deep wisdom that comes from the depths of her soul and know that all who read her works will indeed profit from them.

William R. Forstchen Ph.D.
NYT best-selling author

Preface

In life people do things for external stuff all the time! We buy a nice cars, then we put stuff on the cars to make them look better. We buy expensive watches or jewelry just because we can. All those things really do nothing for you. That nice ROLEX will not give you happiness or will not help you with relationships at work or any other relationship for that matter.

Without meditating life is hard to manage. Most people can't even spend five minutes for themselves. Meditating is a way of life. It brings me happiness and puts everything into perspective. It helps clear my mind, relieves stress. Everything is all in the mind... everything.

I live one hour away from the Jersey shore and I try to go to the beach to meditate as much as possible. I don't know what it is about the ocean but for me it's the most relaxing place on planet earth! Yep, I drive 2 hours round-trip to meditate for 20-30 minutes Why? Because it feels great. The sun, the sand, the ocean waves crashing on the shore... I even do it during the winter time. Of course I am not wearing the proper clothing and people think I'm nuts. But if people knew what I get out of meditating on the beach they would not question it! PURE BLISS! Isn't that the goal in life?

I've been a radio personality for over 27 years. It is an extremely stressful occupation. Without Nora's teachings of stress management I would not be able to make it! Guided Visualizations for me are a life changer and Nora's knowledge is second to no one! I can't thank Nora enough for the help she has given me.

CHIO IN THE MORNING
Philadelphia Radio Personality

Introduction: Preventing Stress

Most preventable deaths come from tobacco, improper diet, lack of exercise, excess alcohol, infectious diseases and stress.

Preventive changes can affect the quality and quantity of life if implemented and maintained. There is a preponderance of evidence indicating that we can do more by preventing and staying away from dangerous or risky behaviors than treating after the fact. Prophylaxis is a Greek word meaning to guard or prevent beforehand. This book explores the journey of mind, body and spirit balance.

What are other causes of preventable death? Is a leading cause of death adverse reaction to prescription drugs?

... Research indicates:
America's Healthcare System is the Third Leading Cause of Death. Barbara Starfield, MD (2000) Journal of the American Medical Association.

In spite of the rising health care costs that provide the illusion of improving health care, the American people do not enjoy good health, compared with their counterparts in the industrialized nations. Among thirteen countries including Japan, Sweden, France and Canada, the U.S. was ranked 12th, based on the measurement of 16 health indicators such as life expectancy, low birth weight averages and infant mortality. In another comparison reported by the World Health Organization that used a different set of health indicators, the U.S. also fared poorly with a ranking of 15 among 25 industrialized nations.

Although many people attribute poor health to the bad habits of the American public, Starfield (2000) points out that the Americans do not lead an unhealthy lifestyle compared to their counterparts. For example, only 28 percent of the male population in the U.S. smoked, thus making it the third best nation in the category of smoking among the 13 industrialized nations. The U.S. population also achieved a high ranking (5th best) for alcohol consumption. In the category of men aged 50 to 70 years, the U.S. had the third lowest mean cholesterol concentrations among 13 industrialized nations. Therefore, the perception that the health of the American Public is a result of their negative health habits is false.

Even more significantly, the medical system itself has played a negative role in the health of Americans. According to several research studies in the last decade, a total of 225,000

Americans per year have died as a result of their medical treatments:

- 12,000 deaths per year due to unnecessary surgery
- 7,000 deaths per year due to medication errors in hospitals
- 20,000 deaths per year due to other errors in hospitals
- 80,000 deaths per year due to infections in hospitals
- 106,000 deaths due to negative effects of drugs

Thus, America's healthcare system is the third leading cause of death in the US after heart disease and cancer.

The New England Journal of Medicine explains: "In our view, prudence requires a skeptical view of the tacit assumption that marvelous new treatments for cancer are just waiting to be discovered. The war against cancer is far from over. The most promising approach to the control of cancer is a national commitment to prevention, with a concomitant rebalancing of the focus and funding of research."

It seems the best way toward better quality and quantity of life is by prevention of illness. Mind, body, spirit and balance that does not allow disease to permeate defense systems and to in fact set intention with daily affirmations and guided visualization as a path.

"Take your seat on the shore. Listen to the ancient voice in the waves. Taste the salt of life on your tongue. Run your fingers through the eternal sand. Breathe deeply. If you find yourself worrying about your cell phone and emails, if you find yourself feeling guilty that you should be doing "something important," breathe deeply again. And again. Breathe deeply until every fabric of your being is reminded that this, being here, is your top priority. This is peace. This is wisdom. The work is a means to living, but this is the living."

- Brian Vaszily

MIND

Mastering Tranquility through Guided Visualizations

There is no doubt that many of us experience stress throughout the day in both our personal and professional lives. Sometimes we do not even realize how tense we are until we set aside a moment to sit down and take a personal inventory of how we are feeling.

Do you have a mind racing with thoughts and constant lists of tasks that need to be accomplished? Do you notice areas of your body that are constantly tense? Are you living in a perpetual state of stress? Stress can have a variety of harmful effects on the body and mind from depression, anxiety, sleep disorders, headaches, ulcers and some even suggest cancer. We have looked at the physiological effects of the fight or flight stress response in detail in my book, *Mastering Tranquility*.

It is well documented that stress has a profound impact on the health of the body and mind. As an example, let's take a look at the number one killer in the United States for both men and women: heart disease. Numerous research studies suggest that the following psychological factors have an impact on the development and progression of heart disease: depression, anxiety, anger and stress (Olivo, Dodson-Lavelle, Wren, Fang,

& Oz, 2009). A study indicated that people with depression are more than two times as likely to experience a cardiac event (such as heart attack, surgery or death) than a not depressed individual (Carney, Saunders, Freeland, Stein, Rich, & Jaffe, 1995). One way to turn the tides of this terrible disease process, and all others related to fight or flight stress is to prevent it before irreversible damage is done.

It is time to claim back our lives and bring ourselves into harmony with a natural state of healing and well-being that can be accessed by anyone. A mind and body that is constantly bombarded with stress signals a stimulation of the sympathetic nervous system which never has time to recover. Eventually, it is as if we become carried away by the momentum of stress, and we forget how to be any other way.

Taking time throughout the day to go into an opposite state of relaxation, rest, calm and happiness reminds our body that there is more than one way to be. The goal is to turn the momentum in the other direction. Let's attempt to make calm our baseline, the norm to which our body always returns.

Challenging situations will always arise and stress in certain situations can be a healthy way to keep us focused on handling a problem or accomplishing a task. However, once the challenge is over, many bodies fail to return to a restful state because we are so accustomed to stress and anxiety. In order to accomplish this baseline of tranquility, we must immerse ourselves in activities that bring about this state of rest.

One technique that has proven to be especially effective in the area of stress reduction is meditation through guided visualizations. Meditation has become a very popular buzz word in the United States as people search desperately for ways to bring their lives back into balance and mitigate the effects of stress on their minds, bodies and spirits.

Some forms of meditation instruct practitioners to bring single pointed focus to their breath or to a mantra, a short phrase that is repeated over and over. It can be difficult to sustain this type of practice because our minds have become accustom to racing with a variety of thoughts and our bodies are programed for productivity.

While mindfulness and mantra meditation, if practiced consistently throughout one's life, can certainly bring about calm and insight, many end up abandoning the practice before they are able to realize any of the potential benefits. One reason for this may be that it is simply a difficult way to accomplish the goal of mastering tranquility. An alternative of guided imagery is not very different from mantra meditation, in a sense.

The purpose of mantras is to keep the mind focused and to perhaps guide the practitioner towards transcendental states through forgetting oneself and breaking past the boundaries of the ego-mind. Why does a mantra necessarily have to be one phrase? Could a mantra not be an entire guided visualization meditation? This would serve a similar purpose.

Guided visualizations bring the mind into single pointed concentration, allowing distractions of a racing mind to drop away. In fact, guided visualizations can be even more effective in achieving this end because it engages the mind, body and spirit in an all-inclusive journey. Guided imagery calls all of the senses together by leading one into a scenario where sight, sound, smell, touch, action, feeling and emotion are activated. Engaging the entire body enhances the ability to sustain a concentrated state.

Mirror Neurons
& Guided Visualization

Scientists have recently discovered mirror neurons. As we change our brain functioning through awareness, we change the energy of the brain and how information is transferred. This is an example of the mind/body/spirit connection. It builds an argument for neurological concept of prayer, wishful thinking and attunement.

The nature of our thoughts set intention.

MRI's have shown that the human inferior frontal cortex is active when the person performs an action and also when the person sees another individual performing an action. A mirror neuron is a neuron that fires both when a person acts and when the person observes the same action performed by another. So, the neuron mirrors the behavior of the other, as though the observer was itself acting. This gave me the idea to include a visualization of action or sometimes an actual visualization on a DVD during my guided meditations.

From SEEDMAGAZINE.COM *June 25, 2012:*

"Mirror neurons continue to light up neuroscientists' imaginations, as several new studies show that the nerve cells respond to more than just visual stimuli. Neuroscientists provide evidence that mirror neurons are multimodal—they are activated by not just by watching actions, but also by hearing and reading about them. An effort led by Lisa Aziz-Zadeh, a neuroscientist at the University of Southern California, found that the brain's premotor cortex shows the same activity when subjects observe an action as when they read words describing it."

Edgar Allan Poe was aware of this long before neuroscience existed…

From *THE PURLOINED LETTER*
by Edgar Allan Poe
(1845)

Nil sapientiae odiosius acumine nimio. - Seneca.
"I fashion the expression of my face, as accurately as possible, in accordance with the expression of his, and then wait to see what thoughts or sentiments arise in my mind or heart, as if to match or correspond with the expression."

The Power of Mental Imagery

One reason why guided visualization is so powerful and effective in stress reduction is related to the mirror neurons. This fascinating concept was discovered by accident in the 1980s by a scientist named Giacomo Rizzolatti. While conducting tests on monkeys, he realized that some of their motor neurons responded in the same way whether they were picking up a piece of food themselves or watching another person pick up a piece of food (Cattaneo & Rizzolatti, 2009).

Subsequent studies on humans using functional neuroimaging supports the theory that these mirror neurons also exist in humans. They are not only located in the motor cortex of the brain which is the area that is responsible for actions, but they are also located in areas of the brain that regulate interpersonal relating, specifically empathy and understanding the intentions of others.

Some have likened the discovery of mirror neurons to Einstein's quantum insights (Duffy, 2009). Just as Einstein's theories rocked the very foundations of Newtonian physics, mirror neurons can be a revolution in neuroscience. What does this mean for those of us who are trying to learn to bring balance into our lives and decrease stress? The implications are amazing. Mirror neurons respond in the same way regardless of whether or not someone is preforming an action or watching an action being performed. What kind of environment do you live in? What types of actions, language and ways of being are you observing in the people around you on a daily basis?

The other day I was working and found that I was feeling very calm, confident and organized. I had to meet with a colleague briefly to discuss our work and she was frantic, frazzled and very anxious about her day. In no time flat I felt stressed, unorganized and hyper about my work and had to take moment to return to a calm center. Why does this occur? It happens because without any cognitive thought on my part, mirror neurons in my brain are firing as I watch my colleague run around frantically trying to organize her day. I empathize as though I am having the same experience.

Likewise, do you have friends in your life who are very self-actualized? When we are in the presence of these people, we rise to the occasion and act and speak in a way that is true to who we are, with wisdom and virtue. Research in mirror neurons suggests that we can change our lives by not only creating skillful habits within ourselves, but also by observing them in others.

This brings us to the topic at hand of guided visualization. Scientists explain that mental images activate processes in the body in a nearly identical way as actually perceiving the objects "in reality". Mental imagery engages certain areas of the brain and then has an effect on the nervous systems. Emotional centers of the brain, particularly the amygdala, will respond. This area is known to play a role in emotions such as anger and fear. There has been much research on the effects of viewing or imagining threatening images. The body will actually respond with an increase in heart rate and respirations (Kosslyn, Ganis, & Thompson, 2001).

Guided imagery has been known to activate the parasympathetic nervous system creating a range of beneficial responses such as reduced anxiety, lowered heart rate and blood pressure, relaxation of blood vessels, slower breathing rate and increased digestion and absorption of food.

One area in which women have been very receptive to using guided imagery is to positively impact their pregnancy. This technique has proven to have positive outcomes in pre-term birth, breast milk production, postpartum depression and self-esteem. Taking medications during pregnancy can have unwanted effects on the fetus and studies are underway to see how effective guided imagery would be in controlling high blood pressure during gestation (Moffatt, Hodnett, Esplen, & Watt-Watson, 2010).

As we are taken on a journey into different landscapes and imagine ourselves doing different actions, mirror neurons are firing as if we are truly in that place, doing those actions, and feeling those feelings. Our motor cortex is stimulated by the activity and the emotional centers of our brain are activated as we empathize with or understand the intention of the visualization. The variety, depth and breadth of inward journeys that we can take are unlimited.

The guided visualizations that you encounter in this book may sound different from others you have heard. Just as in my book, *Mastering Tranquility*, these visualizations were created very intentionally to take you on a particular journey. You may be able to relate to some better than others. Some may not appear to be particularly calming initially, but go along for the ride to see what comes up for you. Perhaps there are some emotions that need to move or be released. Regular practice and use of guided visualizations will have a calming effect on your body and mind that will enhance your natural capacity for healing and vitality.

References:

Carney, R., Saunders, R., Freeland, K., Stein, P., Rich, M., & Jaffe, A. (1995). Association of depression with reduced heart rate variability in coronary artery disease. *American Journal of Cardiology, 76(8)*, 562-564.

Cattaneo, L., & Rizzolatti, G. (2009). The mirror neuron system. *Archives of Neurology, 66(5)*, 403-406.

Duffy, J. (2009). Mirror neurons and the reenchantment of bioethics. *The American Journal of Bioethics, 9(9)*, 2-4.

Kosslyn, S., Ganis, G., & Thompson, W. (2001, September). Neural foundations of imagery. *Nature Reviews Neuroscience, 2*, 635-642. Moffatt, F., Hodnett, E., Esplen, M., & Watt-Watson, J. (2010, December).

Effects of guided imagery on blood pressure in pregnant women with hypertension: A pilot randomized controlled trial. Birth, 37(4), 296-304.

Olivo, E., Dodson-Lavelle, B., Wren, A., Fang, Y., & Oz, M. (2009, October). Feasibility and effectiveness of a brief meditation-based stress management intervention for patients with or at risk for coronary heart disease: A pilot study. *Psychology, Health & Medicine, 14(5), 513-523.*

Strength of the Mind

In an article published in the *Journal of Neurophysiology*, entitled "Strength increases from the motor program: comparison of training with maximal voluntary and imagined muscle contractions," scientists G. Yue and K.J. Cole divided subjects into two groups: (1) Subjects that performed strength training exercises for the pinky finger, five times per week, and (2) subjects that visualized performing the same exercise, but did not physically move their pinky fingers. The visualization group was even hooked up to an electromyography device that measured skeletal muscle contractions to ensure they weren't tensing or otherwise engaging the muscles during periods of visualization. After four weeks, both groups were tested. The group that performed the exercises increased their strength by 30%. The group that only visualized the exercises increased their strength by 22%, an impressive improvement.

An excerpt from the study's abstract:

"Strength increases can be achieved without repeated muscle activation. These force gains appear to result from practice effects on central motor programming/planning. The results of these experiments add to existing evidence for the neural origin of strength increases that occur before muscle hypertrophy."

Source: AJP - JN Physiology May 1992 vol. 67 no. 5 1114-1123

Visualization To Prepare For a Workout

A few minutes prior to exercising, find a quiet place. Gyms aren't known for their serene atmospheres, so before walking inside, simply recline in the front seat of your car and shut your eyes. The entire process should take about three to five minutes.

Slow your breathing and direct your attention inward. Shut off both internal and external noise and pay attention to the present moment. If unwelcome thoughts come into your head, let them pass by just as quickly as they arrived.

Are there any areas that have yet to recover from previous physical activity? Pay attention to any part of the body that is tight or sore as to better notice how it will respond during warm-ups.

Eliminate any negativity and replace it with objective assessment. Evaluate how your body is feeling. Are you still experiencing systemic fatigue from too much activity, too little sleep, or poor dietary choices? Central nervous system fatigue can cause neurotransmitters to function less efficiently, which means that muscle fiber recruitment (and therefore, strength) could be less than optimal. An intense workout in a fatigued state could be counterproductive in the long term if it leads to complications from over-training, which are basically the same as over-stressing yourself in other areas, and can lead to pronounced fatigue, sleep disturbances, appetite changes, anxiety and depression.

Briefly visualize each of the exercises that you intend to perform during your workout. See yourself successfully completing the desired repetitions with perfect form.

Slowly return to full awareness of your surroundings.

Outdoor Fitness

Walk or Run: 30 minutes at moderate effort.

Attempt to complete this walk/run by breathing only through your nose. If you're forced to begin using an open mouth to take in oxygen, then slow down to an intensity that will allow you to utilize only nose-breathing. Working at this level of effort will minimize the amount of time it takes your body to recover between exercise sessions and allow you to experience the great outdoors more regularly, while still providing a steady increase in your overall fitness level. Progress by gradually increasing the distance covered in the 30-minute sessions.

Squats: 2-3 sets of maximum repetitions.

Stand with your feet shoulder width apart and extend the arms forward to help keep balance. Bend at the hips and knees and lower yourself until the thighs are parallel with the ground (or as close to this as flexibility allows). Keep a level back without rounding. Keep your heels flat on the ground and shins as vertical as possible, ensuring your knees don't extend past your toes. From the bottom position, push yourself back up using power from your legs.

Push-ups: 2-3 sets of maximum repetitions.

Lie face down on a clean surface (it may be wise to use a yoga mat) with your hands under your shoulders and your feet about shoulder width apart. Keeping the legs and core straight and tight, push yourself up until your arms are straight at the top. Then lower yourself back down under your chest lightly touches the floor.

Repeat workout 2-3 times per week.

Restoration

Each day, I make it a point to step away from my computer screen, turn off the television and slip on a pair of sneakers to head outside. Often accompanied by my faithful canine companion "Millburn", these walks offer me a brief moment to reconnect to life, to step outside my small dramas and to forget the stress of working life. Sometimes these walks are more like brief runs through the rain. Other times, when I am fortunate, they are long meandering hikes in the mountains and around my favorite lakes and streams.

Even 15 minutes outside can be restorative. Whether I conceptualize it or not, it is difficult to remain enmeshed in my own stress when I look up at the vast blue sky, watch the trees wave in the breeze or smile as my dog scampers through puddles. Life is living, growing and changing all around me. It has done so for a very long time and will continue long after I am gone. There is something very reassuring in this experience.

"I follow nature as the surest guide, and resign myself with implicit obedience to her sacred ordinances."

Marcus Tullius Cicero (Tully) (106-43 B.C.) - Cicero: the Orations translated by Duncan, the Offices by Cockman, Volume 3, Cato: Or, An Essay on Old Age

Natural Landscapes

There is a reason why all of the guided visualizations in this book take the reader to natural settings. It is for the same reason that all of the Tranquil Seas Retreats are either in a remote mountain location or by the ocean. In fact, in some of the locations it may be difficult to get cell phone service. As a society, we have moved far away from our origins as a species that used to live in harmony with nature. Our eyes are bombarded by images on one electronic screen or another for the majority of the day, whether it is a computer, television, iPhone, or Nook. Our friends are little icons on our Facebook page with a profile and lots of nice pictures of their family and an endless supply of comments about what social engagements they may be attending at the moment.

This massive amount of audio-visual stimulation, electromagnetic fields, and the use of artificial light has our bodies utterly confused and out of touch with the natural rhythms of the earth. It is no wonder that so many suffer from sleep disorders. The body used to take its cues from rising and setting of the sun and the changing of the seasons. Hormones are naturally released into the body by the pituitary gland that prepares the body for sleep. As we push this timing back by staying up in front of the television and working on the computer late into the night, the adrenal glands then kick in. The body needs to stay awake somehow, and cortisol does the trick. As you may remember from my book, *Mastering Tranquility*, cortisol is a stress hormone. Constant circulation of this hormone can have deleterious long term effects on many body systems, from digestion to cardio-vascular. In terms of sleep, cortisol is certainly not a hormone that will help in that department. It also circulates in the body for many hours. This can sometimes cause one to wake in the middle of the night or early in the morning and have difficulty returning to sleep.

Despite the fact that the television barrages the senses with millions of images and sounds at an alarmingly fast rate, it is a very passive, one dimensional form of stimulation.

Nature, on the other hand, engages all of our senses and has the ability to have a profoundly calming effect on the body and mind. In his book *Last Child in the Woods,* Richard Louv brilliantly coins the phrase "nature-deficit disorder". Though this is not an official medical or psychological diagnosis, it very aptly describes a problem that plagues many in our fast paced modern society.

While I do not need science to tell me that nature has many restorative and calming effects on all humans from child to adult, it is amazing to see the results of some research in this area. In a country where many people are feeling very overworked and stressed, employers are attempting to find ways to create more healthy work environments. It is costly to have employees who are frequently calling out from work due to illness. A whole host of interventions have been tried from playing soothing music, to having plants and small waterfalls in the office to hanging pictures of beautiful nature scenes on the walls.

Findings from a 2011 study showed that direct contact with nature was most strongly associated with stress reduction and the overall health of employees in an office setting (Largo-Wight, Chen, Dodd, & Weiler, 2011). Considering the potential for stress related illness, it would be beneficial for all of us to incorporate time in nature into our daily routine just as we would attempt to eat enough fruits and vegetables.

It has been found through research that when children spend time in nature, a whole host of positive effects can be noticed. Children who play in natural settings have been found to have superior motor coordination and increased ability to pay attention in school. When children play on a playground with a blacktop with a jungle gym, their interactions tend to be less imaginative and more competitive. Those who are more physically adept tend to dominate. When play is moved to a green setting with grass, trees and rocks, children engage in far more imaginative games with elaborate plots that often continue over the course of several days. Play is far more cooperative and children who are more intellectually creative rise as the natural leaders.

Children with attention deficit disorder who spend more time playing outside in green spaces have seen a decrease in their symptoms and an increased ability to concentrate (Taylor & Sullivan, 2001).Working or going to school in a setting that has windows with a view of nature improves the ability to concentrate for longer periods of time and eases stress. On the other hand, activities such as watching television and playing video games increase the symptoms of ADHD. As a young teacher specializing in children with ADHD I knew instinctively that taking my class to an open green field or a long walk down by a stream was far more effective than any other types of behavior modification or medications. Their academic achievement was far superior upon our return consistently on the days we went out into nature. I also participated in the Pocono Environmental Education week away in the mountains with all of my classes. The skills of orienteering, hiking, study of the ecology and natural habitat of the various plants and animals of the region was the highlight of the academic school year, for me and the kids!

Think back to your childhood play experiences. In nature, our imagination has room to take flight. The open space gives us a sense of calm. Whether we intellectualize it or not, we are put in touch with the fact that life is bigger than our little worlds. Games in green spaces are full of mystery and adventure. Rocks become a castle and a small patch of trees is a jungle. As adults, we may not play in nature the same way we did as a child, unless we are blessed to be in the presence of young children who insist that we partake in their imaginary worlds, but we experience similar benefits. Or, unless we are raised from birth being taught the value of spending time in the great outdoors as I was. At a young age, probably around three, my father took me to the local park and placed me on the icy lake with my first skates. I went ice skating almost daily for the entire winter and then learned the joy of summer swimming, fishing and canoeing in the lakes. The park also presented hours of physical activity hitting tennis balls against a back board and finally tennis court in the sun and the fresh air. As a family we went hiking in the woods and Nordic skiing in wonderful new areas in Vermont, New Hampshire and Maine. Life in California provided trips to the mountains and long walks on the beach exploring tide pools and boogie boards.

My interest in nature is based on years of observation, exploration, personal experience and now scientific evidence to substantiate the benefits. As with anything, there is a time and place for electronics. I certainly do not advocate that we toss our computers and Nooks into the lake. I own a Nook, Kindle, Blackberry, iPhone and many computers and love them! Remaining in a place of moderation and creating balance in our lives is at the core of my teachings.

Keep In Mind...

Silencing the mind by meditative concentration is increased by the silence creating the inner peace that opens the door to one-pointed meditation. While meditating we target something for the mind to concentrate on, which will give tranquility. The targeted effects of reciting a mantra, watching a candle burn, visualizing a cresting wave over and over again, or simply concentrating on breathing creates the environment for serene meditation from consciousness to super consciousness. One should start with ten minutes a day, and progress to twenty.

Meditation is usually performed regularly in the morning and evening. It may be performed alone, or in a group. It involves sitting in silence with the back straight and centered, keeping the body still, taking deep breaths, and keeping the mind still. Seated meditation is a practice of sitting in stillness that ultimately allows us to experience a higher awareness. During the day's activities, try to remind yourself to keep proper posture with the back, similar to the posture taken when meditating. This helps keep focus on the activity at hand, and the effort of engaging in good posture helps quiet the mind during a stressful day.

The calming effects of meditation can impact you positively both mentally and physically by reducing stress, increasing energy and enhancing mental clarity. Meditation focuses the mind's attention on a certain thought or feeling. Accordingly, when meditating focus on what you want, not on what you don't. Keep an inward mental focus. Focus allows the mind to concentrate without interference from other outside thoughts. Looking inward can help improve your connection with the external world. Visualization focuses the mind's attention on an act or movement, making a connection between the imagination and subconscious.

Quick Start Guide
To Meditative Visualization

Find a quiet place.

Eliminate distractions such as cell phones, television, and computers.

Get comfortable.

Choose a comfortable position, preferably one of the following:
- Upright on a chair
- On a cushion
- Cross-legged
- Lotus or Half-Lotus posture
- Burmese seated position, one leg in front of the other
- Kneeling, with the posterior on a bench or supported by cushion

Keep a straight back.

Focus your attention on breathing or a Mantra. A mantra can be a poem, prayer, phrase, chant, or word.

Center breathing on the Hara line (the line that runs vertically up the center of the body).

If the mind wanders, bring it back to your breath or mantra.

Focus on positive thoughts and/or visualize a tranquil setting.

It may be helpful to set a timer if so desired when it is time for you to re-enter full consciousness.

Guided Visualizations

The guided meditations in this book are intended to be read aloud to an individual or group by a facilitator.

Lie down on your towel or yoga mat and find a happy place.

Tune out the outside world and draw senses inward by bringing attention to the breath. Scan the body.

Detach from stressful thoughts and from negativity.

You are not your thoughts, but a calm presence.

When the meditation is over, lie in silence for a few minutes.

Guided Visualization:
Magnificence of the Magnolia Tree in Bloom

Photo: Barbara Snow

Magnificence of the Magnolia Tree in Bloom

By March the snow is dirty on the sides of the road and the piles of ice in the shopping mall lots simply nasty to navigate. On Groundhogs Day Puxitawny Phil predicted six more weeks of winter. The warmth of the spring sun will soon appear with longer days and the end of icy roads.

The spring equinox brings with it the rebirth we crave when things simply begin to become oppressive. With each March the weather comes in like a lion still hovering between winter and summer. The winds are cold and the rain icy and damp and just when we can't stand it the morning sun burns bright and the warmth is powerful. The skies turn blue with clear weather clouds and it is on that day we know the spring is almost here. Winter ends in the east as quickly as it begins.

Open the door to the great outdoors and feel the warmth of the first spring breeze. Enter the yard to explore the joys of nature during the transitional season of rebirth. The fragrant scents of the season pound the sense of smell. The honeysuckle is over powering walking near the long line of shrubs with beautiful white flowers hanging waiting to be picked and tasted by pulling the pistol and its nectar from each flower.

The magnificence of the magnolia trees and the pink flowers entices us to climb up into the arms of the branches as we did as kids, innocent and loving the gentle scent from the flowing petals.

The buds from the dogwood will blossom into the pinks and whites of cross like structures. Small but mighty trees with the spiritual wonders of hope.

Walking slowly across the yard the buds on the huge oaks are ready to burst open with the promise of a new day, a new season, another chance.

Popping out of the ground still cold from the winter ice is the crocus, first out and proud of it. Crocus is followed by the pansies, daffodils and impatience. Warm rains help to encourage the spring growth.

Everything about this warmth of the spring season prepares us for the joys of planting, weeding and watering. Encourage it. The herbs come first with careful preparation of the pots. Parsley will stand up to the cool nights so it is planted first, then the mints as we almost taste them in our teas and meats. Finally the basil, which needs more sun and warm summer nights or it will not survive. Tending to the wildflowers and roses and rhododendron shrubs balances out the gardening, some fruits... some vegetables... some herbs. Variety is the spice of gardening and the garden comes alive in the spring.

Pruning the roses, digging a plot for tomatoes and eggplant, trimming the azaleas we are outside in the fresh air enjoying the nurturing rays of the sun. Mowing the lawn and smelling the fresh cut grass, walking back and forth making beautiful lines as we follow the mower is meditative, as valuable as a walking meditation.

Up and down back and forth forgetting the mental chatter, the problems at the office, the decisions that need to be made, just being here and now in the present. Walking thru the gardens preparing and seeding is in the now. Notice the blue jays chattering, the cardinals and scarlet tanagers brighten up the vibrant colors of nature and the little chipmunks making churpy sounds as they run and scamper about preparing for the new life of this spring.

At the end of this wonderful outdoor adventure every muscle in our body feels like it was used and stretched and we know that sleeping well tonight is a sure bet!

Guided Visualization:
The Pesse Canoe Glides

Photo: Kip Hoffman

The Pesse Canoe Glides

A canoe glides through the water with a serene calmness... the canoe is a boat dug from a pine log... like the first boat ever used... it was called the Pesse canoe in 8000BCE... Pesse... a serene word to describe a serene glide... my visual is of the majestic colors of the white and grey birch... floating down a slow moving steam... with my hand dangling in the water...

The stern paddler is responsible for steering the canoe... the paddle blade is forward alongside and dipped into the water and then drawn back...

The splash of the paddle in the water is calming, rhythmic and meditative. The canoe glides through the water past the honey suckle on the shore, under the Spanish moss hanging from the Bald Cypress and Southern live oak, the trees providing shade from the direct sun.

Allow your hand to hang down over the side of the boat and feel the cool lake water run through your fingers.

Now look over the side into the crystal clear water as the small mouth bass and trout swim around sucking vegetation for nourishment, spitting it out, sucking more in. Feel the tension begin to diminish and the blood pressure drop and heart rate become regular.

5, 4, 3, 2, 1.

Now exhale.

Your body is releasing tension.

Feel your jaw relax and your shoulders sink down into the mat, your legs feel as if you are floating.

Inhale cool air and fill your body.

Exhale the tense hot air you have been holding.

Your body is totally relaxed.

Replace negative thoughts with positive affirmations.

Set your intention to climb up and out of your stressful existence.

Guided Visualization:
Down The Jersey Shore

Photo: Barbara Snow

Prepare for the meditation by getting comfortable. Wear clothes that are easy to rest in and feel just right. Sit up with your feet touching the floor or lie down flat on a yoga mat and start by crossing your arms so your hands are resting on the front of your shoulders. This hand position means victory over ignorance, hate and violence. Set your intention for good thoughts, good words, good deeds. Get still. Now, place your hands and arms in a comfortable position. Close your eyes and take three deep breaths and begin.

Down The Jersey Shore

The sound of the waves crashing against the jetty precedes the sight of the sea. Walking through the dunes, you can hear and smell the ocean before your feet touch the sand and you place your chair in the perfect position. Open the chair and drop your towel. Spread the beach blanket down on the warm white east coast sand. On this day it seems as white as salt.

As you sit and get comfortable look up at the gorgeous white cumulus clouds in the perfectly powder blue sky. They are fluffy like cotton and inform us the sun will shine all day.

The sun's rays permeate the organs of your body and hit every inch of exposed skin. Feel the warmth. Feel the power of the Vitamin D you absorb and its healing energy.

The waves continue to crash creating white caps as high as the boardwalk. The pounding of those waves creates both an excitement and anticipation of becoming one with the sea. Reach for your boogie board now and get up from your chair and start walking toward the sea. Walk faster and then a little faster. Now run at top speed the way you did as a small child knowing you were safe and loved by the family and friends who took you to the beach. Run into the sea kicking past the small white caps and jumping them crashing into the waves head on. Place your body on the board in preparation for the ride in. Turn you head just enough to see the perfect curl of the wave that will carry you all the way in to shore.

You feel as if you are floating now as you ride the surf with not a care in the world. No past. No future. Just right now in the present and the closest you will come to levitating.

Standing up after that wonderful ride pick up the board and charge back in repeating that first with the boogie board and then getting adventuresome and body surfing in many more waves until your body feels fully alive with a tranquility that you set as your intention.

Walk softly back to your beach towel and place your body flat down with your eyes closed and resting in a yoga-like Savassana.

Think of nothing, just feel.

Feel the joy of knowing you are safe and loved and happy in your choices.

Feel the sun again to work its miracle, natures healing rays. Smell the fish and ocean scents. Taste the salt on your lips.

Listen to the sounds of the waves moving in and out with the flow of the tides and believe that this is the moment you need to take with you back into the world where we live our lives. Knowing that you have the power to master tranquility.

Guided Visualization:
Majestic View of the Snow-Capped Mountain

Photo: Kip Hoffman

Majestic View of the Snow-Capped Mountain

Prepare for a meditative journey high above the Blue Ridge Mountains where the lenticular clouds hover like a massive dome over the Kittatinny range.

Calm your body and refocus your mind lie face up with your hands and legs relaxed and your head and neck on a pillow.

Focus on your breath, only the breath let thoughts go. Inhale, exhale...inhale, exhale....inhale, exhale....inhale and hold it.

5, 4, 3, 2, 1.

Now exhale.

Your body is releasing tension. Feel your jaw relax and your shoulders sink down into the mat, your legs feel as if you are floating. Inhale cool air and fill your body. Exhale the tense hot air you have been holding.

Your body is totally relaxed.

Replace negative thoughts with positive affirmations.

Set your intention to climb up and out of your stressful existence.

Visualize yourself floating on a soft white cumulous cloud. It is cotton like and puffy and looks like cauliflower. It is the fair weather cloud and a nice place to be. Living our lives in calmness and fair weather. Visualizing the serenity of equanimity and loving kindness. Hold on to your cloud and be safe, protected from all the ups and downs that the pressure of life toss at us.

Hold on and experience the tranquility of your ride as a place you want to be in this lifetime.

You are rising up now as your cloud moves higher relaxed and resting with your arms and legs stretched out and floating. Look at the panoramic view of the mountain range. Looking up to see the nimbus and cirrus clouds. The gray covering that appears to be curling locks of hair almost in ringlets is misting with a slight drizzle.

As in life when we are faced with the fog we hold tight to our fair weather cloud and move forward. Now in view the rain snow sleet and hail from a dark nimbus high about the horizon but it passes quickly if we maintain the evenness of equanimity. We visualize ourselves holding our place on the fair weather cloud and break through the storms to the majestic view of the snow-capped mountain range. Open your heart and eyes to nature's beauty.

Enjoy the ride with gratitude for the ability to see and feel and smell the wondrous sights of a magnificent mountain range. Gratitude for what we do have. Gratitude for our good health and love of family and friends.

Ride down now on your tranquil cloud to the bottom of the mountain to a calming visual of resting near a beautiful stream that is filled by the snow running off the mountain. Feel the safety of the ground beneath you and knowing you are firmly grounded to earth's magnetic core. Grounded, in survival skills that serve you in life in the day to day trials and tribulations. Grounded in your ability to maintain balance in the face of any adversity.

Begin to slowly stretch as you sit up to take a last look at the serene stream flowing gently past your feet.

Move your fingers and wiggle your toes. Open your eyes and breathe deeply.

From the seated position rise slowly and stand tall.

Raise your hands up toward the mountain toward the sky and say "I am grateful for my good health and love of family and friends"

Guided Visualization:
Snowing Like A Russian Novel

Photo: Kip Hoffman

Snowing Like A Russian Novel

It's snowing like a Russian novel with freezing temperatures, but you move forward because today is the day you will Nordic ski.

Feel the wind and ice forming on your face and every area of exposed skin. Walk slowly toward the paths available in the clearing.

North will take you down a trail of prepared pites or parallel groves cut in the snow. It is neatly cut by machines and frequently the choice of the cross country skier.

South heads out into a mountain of snow untouched by anything except nature. The choice is obvious. With the full realization that opening a track through deep snow can be arduous you move forward, placing your snow boots into the ski and picking up your poles.

The basket at the end of each pole assures you that you won't sink too deeply into the beautiful white powder.

The poles pushing off of the classic ski motion, left leg push right pole, right leg push left pole. Rhythmic, repetitive motion gliding with each stride releasing endorphins and keeping you in the now.

The poles for steadiness and propulsion feel like extensions of your arms and move with you as extended limbs.

Rhythmic, pulsating, gliding forward on flat terrain up and down small hills without breaking the stride of this walking meditation. Left, right, left, right there is no thinking now only the beautiful cadence of the rhythm. If you are thinking you are not meditating.

Feel the pulse of the motion and the joy of being out in the natural beauty of the winter forest.

See your breath as you exhale in the cold crisp air, and feel the rhythm of your breathing in sync with the movement of the skis.

You are alone and at peace with your solitude. The isolation and lack of communication is growing on you as you leave the sounds of the city behind. They are exchanged with sounds of winter birds chirping, little red foxes looking out from behind their hutches and magnificent bucks with brown shaggy fur snorting like ponies.

The smells of the forest are overwhelming with the heightened senses in this environment. All of the cabins have cedar aroma from burning logs in their fireplaces. Breathe in the beauty and breathe out the stressors. There is a familiar smell of family and fun and a spiritual awakening from the pine forest, bringing up memories of joyful Christmas aromas.

Breathe in the joyful scents and breathe out the mental disquietude.

Stop for a rest and sip nourishment from your water bottle. Replenish your cells with the fluid of life. Value the moment and allow yourself to be happy. Relish the moment as feeling really alive with gratitude for who you are and what you have. Prepare to climb the hill in front of you as there will always be hills and valleys in life. Spreading your skis out so they look like the letter V, herringbone up the hill with a passion to reach the other side, feeling a sense of accomplishment as your reach the crest.

Take a deep breath, hold it… counting down from five, four, three, two, one…

Push off to glide down the hill at a faster speed pointing your skis inward to snowplow and control your descent. Acceptance that change is inevitable for the rest of this ride because at the bottom is a frozen lake. Hitting the lake at full speed in the skating motion of the cross country skier allows you to change on a dime as is often the case with the trials and tribulations of life.

Pushing first with the right leg as an ice skater and shifting all of your weight to the right leg you find your cadence once again and soon settle in with a feeling of balance and grace gliding through life and across the large lake to the other side. Transfer your weight to control the glide and slide into the snow completing the journey with a feeling of success, a joyful job well done and the serenity of the meditation known as mastering tranquility.

Guided Visualization:

Vibrational Level Up After the End of a Relationship

Photo: Kip Hoffman

Vibrational Level Up After the End of a Relationship

We will raise our vibrational levels getting more in touch with the stressors that life brings.

Eyes closed and take your fingers and smooth out your eyebrows.

Feel the temporomandibular joint by placing your fingers in the middle of your cheek. Now gently open your mouth, if pain comes you carry stress in the TMJ joint. Gently open your mouth and make an effort to do so rather than clenching.

Breathing in thru the nose and out thru the nose as nature intended. The filters in the nostrils helping to purify in the natural rhythm. The mouth is for eating not breathing. Shoulder shrugs first forward and then toward the back.

Take your fingers and place one in between each toe bending them back and forth in a rhythm and flow. Prepare for the day......your first day alone since the break-up....with the realization that the break up process is a lonely experience unequalled in life by any other single event except death of a loved one.

Visualize yourself in a child's pose yoga position then slowly opening up like a flower in the spring. Slowly pulling up your arms standing then moving into full tree pose.

This visualization is a symbolic metamorphosis... coming up and out of the emotional pain of the breakup.

Say the words I will survive and prosper.

I will survive and prosper.

In each relationship one partner has one foot out the door alternating with the other partner in any given year. Acceptance of the break up as a final event is the first step.

See yourself detaching. It is our attachment that causes suffering.

When it no longer exists step back as an observer... be grateful for what you had that is gone...

Reflect on the joys and sorrows the best and worst of times and accept the entire process as a learning experience.

Saying, I will survive and prosper and triumph!

I will survive and prosper and triumph.

The exit of a partner who does not want to share your life is a blessing. I will survive and prosper and triumph.

Hold no ill will and let go of the past. Avoid the triggers that cause pain. Hold the positive image of the rest of your life as serene and healthy and all that you deserve.

"I will survive and prosper and triumph."

Tune out the outside world and draw senses inward by bringing attention to the breath. Scan the body. Detach from thoughts and from negativity. You are not your thoughts, but a calm presence.

Rejoice in the realization that you are not your relationship...... But rather an amazing human being who will rise up and out of the break-up to better quality of life than you ever dreamed possible. Visualize a phoenix rising and follow its mythical path to a life that is now free to vibrate at a level up.

Guided Visualization:
Principles of the Master

Photo: Kip Hoffman

Principles of the Master

There are several obstacles which preclude spirituality. Included in that list are hate, fear based emotions, indecision, immaturity and arrogance. Usui Reiki principles from Japan serve as a structure to move past these obstacles. The principles do not use the words I, me, mine because they are taken from affirmations that believe in egolessness.

JUST FOR TODAY, DO NOT ANGER.

Place your hands over your eyes, what the eyes don't see the heart doesn't grieve about. Anger might be an evolutionary emotion that has survival value because it keeps you from being taken advantage of from people who want what you have. It is a form of aggression. Release the need for this immature emotion that served generations in the past, but is no longer needed in our civilized and more compassionate world. Realize that it causes a fight or flight reaction and increased cortisol which decreases quantity and quality of life. Visualize a kinder gentler reaction to all of the various triggers that result in what we call anger. See yourself getting cut off on the highway and gently accepting the intrusion by dropping back and decreasing speed and letting him go…… letting go of the anger that hurts only you. Practice equanimity. If we learn not to anger we will be able to show gratitude and showing gratitude to all living things will result in anger not being able to arise. It is imperative to practice what we say we believe.

JUST FOR TODAY, DO NOT WORRY.

Worry shuts down the sacral chakra and stops abundance from flowing into your life. When you stop worrying abundance returns. Create healthy imprints that come in the form of saying something, doing something or even thinking something.

Place hands over temples, the temples are related to the active sides of the brain, therefore using this principle here indicates balance of thoughts and thinking. Worry use to prepare us by anticipating the physical threats of the dinosaur in pursuit. Worry is excessive concern. It has evolved in us to prepare for the potential dangers. Worry about past choices that can't be changed and future calamities that may or may not happen has deleterious affect on our bodies. Visualize a feeling of trust and serenity. See your teen-ager charge the sea with her surfboard and think good thoughts, know that she will soon stand and ride that glorious wave all the way to the shore. Believe in her and accept that biting your nails until bloody will not result in an injury free ride. See the smile on her face and the joy in her aura as she glides in joy and feel pride in her athleticism and training without a care in the world.

HONOR YOUR PARENTS, TEACHERS AND ELDERS

Healing the relationship with parents and elders is more about gaining insight into how those interactions have created imprints in our youth, that to this day cause distress especially people in authority who sent us messages of following their rules or withdrawing love and affection.

Place your hands over back of head. Honor all parents and elders with the full understanding that they did their best job. Reflect back to the structure and discipline they provided to keep us safe and out of harms way. To teach us basic facts and general funds of knowledge. We will journey back in time and visualize the many times mom told us to put on our coat when it was cold outside. The mountain of snow was so inviting and we knew best and wanted to just jump in without all those hats and coats. Without fail we were told we would get sick and the cold and fever followed the joy of the snowball fight. As we got older we really knew it all and told the parents we could not possibly get sick without the coat because germs caused colds. But the elders knew best and the attack of 15 degrees on our immune system did in fact correlate to the colds and the excellent advice of wearing protective clothing. Visualize yourself interacting with the elders in a more trusting and respectful way and the love that creates.

EARN YOUR LIVING HONESTLY.

Place your hands over the throat, the area of communication. Visualize yourself as a young child in a class of faith based study. The regular teacher is absent and the substitute is a jolly man who loves to be teaching that day. He steps up to the lectern and has your undivided attention because from his first words you know this is your first exposure to spirituality. He begins by saying work to your fullest potential whatever the job, feel good about your work and give it 100% every hour of the day. Earn your living honestly and ethically and give it all you have. Do not complain or resent or anger. Do your work, single task and be paid for an honest day of labor. Part of your work is your attitude and spiritual path. End your day with prayer and or meditation.

SHOW GRATITUDE TO ALL LIVING BEINGS.

Place your hands over your heart the area associated with love…

Start this visualization with the smallest living being, bacteria, living in our intestines that make nutrients and process toxins and enable us to digest and for them we are grateful. Breathe in the oxygen produced by plants and trees and yes go out and hug them! See the honeybees pollinating our plants and the joy of our companion dogs and cats jumping on our heads early on a Saturday morning. Hear Grandma Lea saying if you have your health you have everything, I can hear her if I concentrate on those words and then rejoice in the value of that statement. Value life and be grateful for what you have no matter how much or how little. Express your gratitude by writing a gratitude list monthly. Start now in your head listing all of the many living beings you are grateful for.

Guided Visualization:
Tranquil Seas Retreat

Photo: Kip Hoffman

Tranquil Seas Retreat

Imagine yourself sitting on the back porch of a lovely little beach cottage...

The sun, the sand, the beach... they are just steps away.

You can hear the ocean, but can't quite see it over the tall dunes or mounds of sand protecting the beach. You decide to take a walk toward the beach. As you approach the dunes you remove your shoes.

Feel the warm sand...it is so soft.

Your feet and toes sink into the warmth...

Continue to walk up the dunes toward the rushing sound of the waves. Hear the ebb and flow of the waves crashing onto the beach...

You've reached the crest of the dunes and are in awe of the beautiful sight.

You find yourself running down the far side of the dunes and onto the beach. The wind is whipping through your hair and onto your face. You feel free... Continue running on the beach. Continue to feel the exhilaration. Run until you can't... You are spent. Your legs are so tired...

You decide to sit down on the sand. Now you lay back in the sand... Ahhhh. You can feel the warmth of the sun beating down upon your face. It seeps into your body. It feels like love....

It touches your heart and continues to touch every cell of your body. You thought you were exhausted from your run, but no, you are feeling energized...

How many times do we feel stressed and say I need a vacation...

Today we will create our own getaway spot, our own little oasis.

Sit quietly and comfortably. Uncross your legs and feet and relax your arms and hands... When you do this on your own you can sit anywhere you would like...on the floor, in a comfy chair, on your sofa or favorite recliner.... Just be sure to not cross your arms or legs so that you allow the energy or chi to flow through your body...

Think about leaving that stressful place you want to escape from. Open the door and walk right out and into a beautiful garden on the other side of the dunes.... It is filled with flowers blooming in vibrant colors.

Under your feet is a cushion of lush green grass. Revel in its beauty. Look around.... Enjoy the view. There is a backdrop of deep green forest.... Off to the side you spot a narrow but well-worn path leading into the trees.

Walk over and enter into the forest.... Continue to walk very slowly.... Hear the soft rustle of the leaves under foot and the spongy bounce from the bed of pine needles.... Feel the love surround you. That canopy of trees will protect you. It will keep at bay the biting winds of winter and shelter you from the rain.... It will shade you from the harsh heat of the summer. This forest is truly beautiful.

Continue walking slowly....

You see a light shining through the trees. Walk toward the light and out into an opening in the trees. Oh, what a beautiful sight. There is a cool refreshing water hole. There is a waterfall bringing water from the snow- capped mountains to fill the water hole.... The water is so cool and clear and refreshing. What a tranquil spot. It's time to create your own tranquil retreat.

Perhaps... it will be a little cottage at the edge of the water, maybe it will be a tree house... Or maybe just a tent...

Find your own little spot and create it. It is your own and no one else can come here and invade your space. You, however, can come here any time you want to find peace. You can calm your mind and your spirit. Remember, this is yours... Revel in its beauty, its peacefulness. Remember this feeling of love and acceptance. This is where you can recharge your battery. Now that you feel refreshed, it is time to go. You are stronger now. You have renewed your spirit. You have filled your being with life giving energy. You are now ready to face your world with renewed vigor.

Close up the "house" that you created. Splash the water in the watering hole one last time. Proceed back into the forest. Remember that feeling of love and comfort that you get from the forest. Begin your journey back through the trees and into the garden. Take another look at the blooming flowers. Soak in the beauty.... Open the door to your world. Enter into it with your head held high, your confidence is evident. You can do anything now. You are renewed.... You will always have your own tranquil seas retreat to energize you. You will be able to go there anytime you want or need to.

Begin to bring yourself back into the here and now. Wiggle your toes and your fingers. Take a deep breath. Open your eyes....welcome home....you are invincible...

Sit for a few more minutes and soak in that wonderful feeling. Remember that feeling of warmth coursing through your body. Remember the feeling of the sun on your face and body. Remember how you felt with the wind whipping at your face. Hang on to that feeling as you get up and begin your slow walk back to your beach house. Remember the feeling of your feet sinking into the warm sand. Walk up and over the dunes again and back onto the porch. You are so very happy. You are content. You are ready now to face your challenges...

Guided Visualization:
Elevate Thoughts As I Climb Towards the Heavens

Photo: Kip Hoffman

Elevate Thoughts As I Climb Towards the Heavens

"I elevate my thoughts as I climb toward the heavens. Looking down on nature as I gain altitude it is calming and renewing..."

Sitting in the airplane after having done a preflight inspection of the engine and flying surfaces.... after starting the engine to prepare for takeoff and thinking about the glide up to a place of natural beauty...The oil temperature gauge moves slowly into the green area indicating the oil is warm enough for the engine to be run up to full throttle for takeoff.....

Takeoff...exhilarating...Time to make a call on the radio to all other airplanes on the ground and to those in the air about to land: "November8875Mike (N8875M) is taking the active, runway zero one for take-off, departing north.... carefully check to see that no airplanes are on final approach and then increase the throttle enough for the propeller to pull the airplane forward onto the runway. Hard left pressure on the left foot pedal rotates the nose of the plane to the runway heading of 010 and slowly push the throttle all the way forward.....

"I elevate my thoughts as I climb toward the heavens. Looking down on nature as I gain altitude it is calming and renewing..."

The engine revs up to full power with a steady roar and the airplane accelerates down the runway. Balancing foot pressure on the rudder peddles keeps the nose of the airplane pointed directly down the center of the runway...

It's a crisp and clear autumn morning, the air is dense and the airplane points its nose upward almost before we realize we are at takeoff speed. The airplane seems to tell us it wants to fly....

Pull gently back on the wheel and the airplane points its nose up and virtually jumps into the sky. We think back to just a few weeks ago in the height of summer in the hot and humid air when the airplane behaves sluggishly and seems to struggle to get off the ground.

"I elevate my thoughts as I climb toward the heavens. Looking down on nature as I gain altitude it is calming and renewing..."

And away we go....we look off to the left and watch the ground slowly recedes as we "climb out". The nose of the airplane is high and all we can see ahead is blue sky....

Blue sky...

Natural beauty like nothing else...

Checking the vertical speed indicator, set the climb rate at 500 feet per minute and sit back until the altimeter shows we have reached the cruising altitude for today of 3000 feet....

At that altitude pushing forward on the yoke and watch the earth ahead comes back into view. pulling the throttle back and set the engine rpm's at 2000 per minute.... check the compass for the correct heading, and then for the first time since takeoff .....Look out the front window and enjoy the majestic view...

"I elevate my thoughts as I climb toward the heavens. Looking down on nature as I gain altitude it is calming and renewing..."

On a day like this at 3000 feet we can see thousands of square miles around. It's almost breathtaking. We see a mountain range 70 miles away. We can see several lakes that it would take hours to see individually in a car. We can see many small towns and large numbers of farms which are neatly defined and variously colored. It's beautiful. We pass over small towns. We watch cars driving on bridges over rivers and on large highways. Everything is serene at altitude except the sound of the small airplane engine, but even that almost hypnotizes.

We fly for an hour and then prepare for landing at the airport in Pennsylvania by calling air traffic control there, telling them we have listened to the current weather and are inbound for landing. Prepare for a strait in landing on runway 27. Pull the throttle back to 1500 rpm. The engine quiets down and we start the decent... we float quietly in to the pattern, pull the nose up slightly to slow the airplane, set the trim tab and descend slowly toward the runway. When over the threshold of the runway pull off all the power from the engine, pull slowly back on the wheel to further slow the airplane and float down until we hear the chirp of the tires on the runway.

"I elevate my thoughts as I climb toward the heavens. Looking down on nature as I gain altitude it is calming and renewing..."

The exit ramp comes into view, brakes on and turn off the runway. Slowly taxi to the fixed base operator building, stop and shut down the engine. The joy of flying entails everything from planning the flight the night before, doing the preflight inspection of the airplane, starting the engine and checking the instruments, flying to the destination and landing the airplane. All other cares disappear for this short time and allows for complete rejuvenation for the next weeks difficulties.

Every morning in Africa, a gazelle wakes up.
It knows it must outrun the fastest lion or it will be killed.

Every morning in Africa, a lion wakes up.
It knows that it must run faster than the slowest gazelle, or it will starve.

It doesn't matter whether you're a lion or a gazelle when the sun comes up you'd better be running.

(But, unless you're a runner, you won't understand.)

-Anon

Running As Meditation

Running is, without a doubt, one of the most popular forms of exercise in the world. It is now commonplace for marathons in large cities to fill to capacity with over 20,000 participants. Not only is the number of people who participate in marathons increasing, but so is the number of people who finish them. This speaks to the popularity of a pursuit that has as many mental health benefits as physical ones.

Many runners have switched from logging their miles on asphalt to the more scenic experience of nature trails.

Some choose to run in pairs or larger groups because they enjoy the camaraderie or competitive motivation. Others choose to run alone to enhance the mental element that can turn a strenuous activity into a very calming one. The perfect connection between mind and body that occurs during what is affectionately called "Runner's High" becomes attainable in part due to the isolation -- the majority of things that can interrupt us during seated meditation are, quite literally, left in the home. The road, and preferably, the trail, provides the impetus necessary to focus on the breath, focus on the rhythm of the feet, and become completely immersed in physical activity.

Tips on how to meditate while running:

- Follow your breath and attempt to synchronize the movement of your body with the inhalation and exhalation of your lungs.

- Be present in the environment that surrounds you

- Both meditation and running require discipline

- Give up the urge to compete with others, or yourself, and focus on the joy of movement.

- Running becomes an obsession for some because they wish they could go farther or faster. Giving up the urge to do more and replacing it with a commitment to getting more out of each session

- While seated meditation trains one to keep the mind focused on breathing, bringing straying thoughts back to each breath that is flowing out of the lungs is even more important when running. Through meditation it is possible to become keenly aware of the inward or outward world.

- Experience the movement of your body

- Focus on the rhythmic striking of your feet on the ground. Experience nothing but each foot coming into contact with the earth. When thoughts enter the mind, acknowledge them, and then let them go. Bring your attention back to the earth.

- There can be painful, or at least, very uncomfortable aspects of distance running. Anyone who has attempted a marathon will attest to that. Scan your body and pay attention to how you are feeling.

- Be completely present in the surroundings

- Focus completely on the present moment and enjoy the journey

- On long runs, there can be adversity. Pain, fatigue, boredom can all become negative issues.

- Relax your muscles from your toes all the way up to your head

- Bring the mind and body together in harmony

- If your body is telling you to slow down or stop, you must listen. However, don't confuse a message that comes from the mind with one that comes from the body. Bringing your attention back to your breath or the rhythmic percussion of your feet hitting the earth can help you work through mental fatigue.

- During a period of strenuous physical exertion, the mind and body need to work in unison to overcome the discomfort caused by intense movement.

- Visualize the successful completion of your goal. Running a very difficult trail in your mind can help you deal with the challenges you'll face on the real thing.

- Proper breathing is necessary to relax both the mind and the muscles.

- Remove negative emotion from the experience

- Be aware, but at the same time, detached. Know that your inner strength can overcome any external circumstances.

- Don't worry about the miles ahead, only concern yourself with the moment you're in.

- Let the results go and just enjoy the experience.

- For an even more meditative experience, you can use a mantra while running.

- Attempt to experience all the senses of the trail…

When we run we experience a deeper scent of fresh cut grass in the spring, of the oils released by the plants after a rain, the hyacinth's aroma and pine cone smells from a wood burning stove…the ever so subtle smells of pies baking and steaks being grilled on the barbeques and the flowers, oh the glorious flowers in bloom and wonderful joy of those scents stay with us long after the run……..

When we run we feel euphoric, running elicits a flood of endorphins in the brain we feel at peace as the meditative serenity takes us away. We also feel the environmental conditions, the incline in the road, the wind and temperature changes more intensely and the exhilaration of the power we possess.

The view while running is at a faster pace, the Canada Geese overhead in formation moving above the runner but almost with him, the long line of pines acting as a border on the property the runner goes by, the sunrise in the morning is a magnificent view for the runner up at the crack of dawn and enjoying what most of the world never views.

Illustrative Journals

The following journal contributions are submissions from avid runners who wish to share their passion for their sport, their health, and their love of the outdoors.........

Illustrative Journal, by Shawn Acosta

I am an accidental runner. You don't just wake up at the age of 44 one morning and decide to be a runner. Well, I suppose you could but that's not how it happened to me. It takes time and determination or in my case, desperation. I was in a bad place in my life. My life was an endless series of busy nothings just going through the motions of being a wife and mother. I hit a wall somewhere and entered what I have come to call my "7 years underwater" because that's what it felt like. It was sort of numb and in slow motion. Get in the car, take the kids to school, go to market, get food, empty the dishwasher, load the dishwasher. Laundry is never really done unless everyone in the house is naked so life became this endless cycle of repetitive chores. I failed to notice the season's changing. The years passed only by birthdays on a calendar and the Christmas tree going up and coming down. There was no great tragedy that overtook me, not tale of loss or illness just the ignorance that life was precious and there was a whole lot going on around me that I couldn't see.

One day, no different than any other I suppose, the stress of emptiness crushed me. I was reading a book thinking about other cultures, exotic places and how much I wanted to travel and experience the world. My life was the house, the grocery store and the school. I had no hardships. There was no bitter winter to survive on onions alone, no hard battle with cancer to overcome. I had it all. The American dream. A house with 3 kids and 2 dogs and a husband that worked hard.

That afternoon after feeling profoundly guilty for feeling sorry for myself for what I declared "no reason" I took the dogs to the park. I have a large fenced yard that I usually let the dogs out in but men were repairing my fence and I had to take the dogs to the local park to be walked and run around. As I walked to the park, their excitement was building. As I let them off the leash I watched as their happiness soared at just being able to run around and chase each other. Their happiness was contagious. It was a cold day; no one else was at the park so I began to chase the dogs. I felt it. My heart was pumping, the cold air filled my lungs and after 2 minutes I was flushed and exhilarated but had to stop and catch my breath. I was doubled over with a stitch in my side. I hadn't noticed that I had gotten fat and sedentary over the years. I was telling my body to run and it stopped responding. Well, maybe I didn't have it all. I wanted to run with the dogs and my body was laughing at me.

The next day I sent the kids off to school and decided to walk around the block. I was frustrated after coming home from the park the day before and didn't even recognize the woman in the mirror that night after my shower. When did this happen? How had I dressed and put my makeup on everyday and never noticed my face? How did I just accept buying clothes in larger and larger sizes and never take notice of it? I walked around the block, felt tired and went in. It was unsatisfying. It was discouraging. I grabbed a bag of Cheetos and sat down to think about it. I consumed the whole bag without giving any thought to what I was eating. I was just feeling sorry for myself. That turned to anger because I had no real reason to feel sorry for myself. I resolved to walk 4 miles the next day.

So I grabbed a pedometer and headed out into the neighborhood and walked 4 miles. Yes, my boring New Jersey suburban development. It took an hour and 45 minutes. I was sore the next day but I got up and did it again. I kept doing it. Everyday. I used these walks to think about my life. More than once I found myself on a street I didn't recognize and had to think hard to turn myself around to get back home because I was so lost in my thoughts. The next day I ripped the ponytail holder out of my hair and walked with my hair down, feeling the breeze and watching the trees. I can't tell you what prompted me to begin jogging but I jogged till I had to stop and catch my breath. Maybe it was the same emotion that prompts someone to punch a wall. I had my heart pumping in minutes and I could feel the blood in my veins. My lungs grew tight. I heard my heartbeat in my eardrums. I heard my breathing in my nose and out my mouth and I never noticed until that moment how loud my body was. I don't think I had ever tried to listen to it. I watched the trees swaying and I felt alive. Sore, tired and exhausted but alive.

Each day I would jog a little more of the 4 miles but I never deviated from completing my full route even though I had to walk most of it. There came some days that it rained and I would do my 4 miles on a treadmill. I did get some strange looks from people in cars and neighbors but I found running in the rain exhilarating! The sky was different, the trees were bowing down to the wind and I felt a little reckless but alive. It scared me a little. I had my best run time that day. I vowed not to use the treadmill in my house unless a hurricane hit. I began to run in any weather, wind, rain, snow, heat and *running I was*. Before I even noticed it happening I was running the whole route. I came to look forward to the little involuntary twitching movements made in my thigh muscles after a long run. I liked the flushed feeling my face got, the skin on my nose felt different than the skin on my cheeks. It was like experiencing my body on a cellular level. Of course I had felt my skins cells before, I had been burned or felt cold and warmth but this was different. Like the skin cells were tiny little vessels all over me that were filing and emptying at the same time. It was my body, I've had it for 48 years now but the feeling my muscles made and my skin felt all seemed new to me. After a run I began to realize what the expression "bounce in her step" meant. Walking after a run was like bouncing on a trampoline.

There would come a point on very special days around mile 3 where I would sense that I was no longer running but gliding through the air, mind empty and I would just "be." In that moment I felt like the combination of molecules that made up "me" dissolved into the air. "I" didn't exist, "I" was part of everything. I felt nothing while feeling everything. If I tried to re-create that moment I would not find it. It could not be duplicated. Some days I would run hard and try to empty my mind but still it would not come. Maybe if I run slower? Maybe if I try and keep my pace steady? Most days I used my run time to think about life, about the water bill or the mortgage payment or a project the kids had at school and I would catch a glimpse of a squirrel running up a tree or the colors changing in the sky and that moment of nothingness, weightlessness would just transform me. The weightless feeling just seemed to happen when nature distracted me from the thoughts inside my mind. The days that weightless feeling overtook me, even if it was short lived, where my strongest. I felt as if that brief moment of nothingness was like hitting a reset button in my brain. I started to stop thinking inside my head and started being observant of nature around me. The feel of the ground beneath my feet, the slope of a hill, the crunch of the leaves or how did the sun hit the bark on some trees at different times of the day? The days were getting longer when I started training myself to feel nothing. I would notice how the light hitting the leaves would change very slightly each day. Flowers and mosses were growing. Running in fog became my special kind of magic. I listened to the wind and watched the sky for changes. I noticed how many shades of green there are and the different kinds of wildflowers that grew along my run route. I noticed tree branches that grew, and animals scurrying in the undergrowth that I normally would not notice. I felt more connected to the world. I wasn't visiting this environment, I WAS this environment. It was as if I had burst through the surface of the water and I was no longer trapped under the waves. I had resurfaced from my years underwater. Suddenly the lure of the market smells in Istanbul paled in comparison to the section on my route where the air was thick with the scent of Honeysuckle. How had I lived in New Jersey for 17 years and didn't know what Honeysuckle was? I had to look it up on the Internet. On a hot day I could smell the Pine trees oozing their sap. In the winter, especially after a snowfall, it was so quiet that the sound of my breathing was deafening. Instead of noticing the sounds I would dwell on the beauty of the absence of sounds. I liked the feel of rain on my face and the heat of the sun on my skin. My favorite time to run is dusk when you can see the sky turn purple and hear the birds retiring for the night and the change in the world over the course of an hour run is visibly perceptible. I stopped looking at street signs and marked my course by moss covered rocks or tree branches that I was forced to duck under and buckles in the sidewalks from tree roots.

Some days were busy and I couldn't find time to run and soon realized my mood was being affected when I couldn't run. No run equaled grumpy mood. Running soon took over. I found that I was being more productive at home to make time in my day for a run. I was more focused on my daily tasks and I began to do them more efficiently because I had run time or "me" time to look forward to. Run time was just me and the wind and the trees and the sky. Run time ceased being the time of day I spent reflecting on my problems and became the time of day I spent reflecting on just "being." I still didn't view this time spent as "working out." "Working out" was something my girlfriends did at the gym or yoga class.

There have been some unintended side effects of becoming a runner. I became a runner out of frustration and the side effects are much better than a broken hand punching holes in the wall.

Before becoming a runner my life was a black and white canvas. Running was the paintbrush that brought the color back into my world. It altered the way I view life and if I get nothing else out of running it was worth it. Other side effects have been courage, better health and self-confidence. When I started attempting to run, I was a size 18. I didn't enjoy shopping and was forever picking and pulling at my shirts to hide from the fat. I'm now down to a size 6. Some ask what diet plan I used to lose weight, what's the secret? There is no secret. Try moving and not eating when you're bored. I would not be considered thin by any stretch of the imagination. If you are reading this and imaging a tall, thin, lithe woman you could not be more wrong. I am a short, stocky built dark haired Irish Gypsy girl. Think more fireplug than supermodel. I'm fit - not thin. I'm often stopped along my run route and asked what I'm training for.

I'm training for life.

I reward myself with running in 5K's, Mud Runs, Obstacle Races and half marathons. Once I was able to run that 4-mile route and my body stopped laughing at me, I decided to push it to its limits. I can't say I am one of those women that pushes so hard they throw up during a marathon or have blisters the size of Texas on their feet. I don't run to punish my body, but to pleasure it. I push and sometimes get sore, but I have no ambition to compete in an Ironman.

After achieving a certain level of fitness I tried going the gym route with my friends. I found it disheartening to sit in traffic for a half an hour only to hop on a stationary bicycle that went nowhere in a gym full of people. Comparing myself to others there only hurt my wallet and my pride. Running is free. Running is natural. Gyms can be expensive, they smell bad and there are no trees. I have friends that want to run with me but I decline because running is so personal, private and spiritual for me.

I have a sense of humor about my running. You will often find me being chased though the woods by Zombies in a Zombie themed obstacle race in matching tutus with my daughter or being covered in paint at a 5K Color Run. Maybe you will find me crawling under electrified barbed wire in a Mud Run Obstacle 5K. My races are a celebration of my training for life, not my goals.

If you are reading this and thinking "yeah, that's great for her but I can't run" think about this. An acquaintance, a very athletic acquaintance, had suggested running after I had my last child 12 years ago to get back into shape and I laughed and said "no thanks, I am a fat, old chick with asthma, I can't run"... he smiled politely and nodded that he understood but pointed out that everyone is a runner at heart. He said "remember when you were 6 and it wasn't called running it was called playing? Try that." I saw him at a race a year ago and he hugged me and said "wow, you get it now!" Yeah, it's called life and I get it now.

-Shawn Acosta

❧ Illustrative Journal, by Diana Brown

Running – How it "saved" me

How life gets in the way – You are a kid and running is second nature, playing outside without a care in the world. I grew up where we ran all over the neighborhood, you came home when called and dinner was ready or when the streetlights came on. How interesting how when you "grow up" – you forget about the basics. Unless you have a family that instills fitness together – life gets in the way. You go to work; you go home, cook dinner for your family. Next thing you know, it's 10pm at night and you are just sitting down for the day.

Fitness was not really a family priority. We ran and played outside, then when I was a teenager we moved to a farm. Outside life was par for the course…feeding animals, hoeing row of flowers or vegetables. It wasn't really "fitness" – it was "work". Then I joined the military. Running became a necessary "evil" – or so I considered it. I ran just enough to get by. Life marched on, and military requirements for fitness changed through the years. Running for an annual fitness test was just another chore. Work. A distraction to the "real things" I needed to do. Somewhere during all this time of working toward advancing my military career, I lost the true value of "playing outside" and hoeing that row of flowers. Life became driving to work (I traveled pretty far) and a child. I didn't know how to balance my life. I had no windows in my office and thought there had to be more to life.

Sometimes the worst circumstances lead to the best things in life. Preparing for a big inspection at work – there was an "issue" and they needed someone to resolve the issue. Lucky me, I got the assignment. It was something I knew absolutely nothing about and was totally outside my normal job. What was I to do? I had only 42 days to take a process, fix it (it was so broken) and pass the inspection. I didn't know what to do or where to start. During this time, I had to prepare for my annual fitness test. So, on top of everything – out the door I went for my run to ensure I could pass the test. A distraction I did not need right now.

What happened was not what I expected... getting out in nature. Reconnecting with the power of the earth, wind, universe I was relaxing with every step I took. My mind cleared, my stress faded, and I was relaxed for the first time in my life during such stressful circumstances. I started looking forward to my runs. I could brainstorm scenarios to pass the inspection. I was able to connect with nature and feel its power. I noticed the fluffiness of the clouds. The colors of the sky...

it's not just blue – its different shades of blue, purple, pink, orange, yellow, grey, and even white. With each run, I was able to let go of a stuffy office. The grass turns several colors of green, brown, yellow. Birds follow and sing to you. Butterflies play with you. Flowers bloom at the side of the road – just for you. They even bloom close to the dirt so the lawn mower won't touch them. The air smells different too… you can smell a rainstorm, humidity, fog, even lightning. Fun times as a child came back to my memory. Smells brought back these memories of playing in the summer, riding my bike with my sister and father. This was the "life" I was living and wanted to live.

Slowly, I found it wasn't just important that I ran – it was absolutely essential. If I missed a run or blew it off for something seeming "more important" – I regretted it. The stress builds, the attitude worsens and the heaviness comes back. This didn't happen overnight, but was a metamorphosis over time. Listening to my body, knowing when to push and when to take it easy. It's been a slow reconnection with nature and myself. Now, it's a necessity – like food or sleep. My assistant kicks me out of my office on a regular basis. My mood dictates when she does….as it's obvious by my behavior when I miss my runs. Sometimes, I'm forced to run on a treadmill… if so, I position myself so I can see outside… and imagine I am out there feeling the wind in my hair and what I would see out in nature that day.

-Diana Brown

Illustrative Journal, by Heather Imielinski

Today with the scent of trees in my nose, car horns flooding my ears, and the morning breeze making my eyes water, I head out to do what I do best....and that is to take care of my body! But why do we run? Why do some of us continue to workout with the passion that we do? Do we have PR's (personal records) to set, distance or weight goals to reach, and competitors to beat and status to earn. Whatever the reason is, we all run to reach a goal, it is the ultimate achievement motivator.

Some days we leave the watch at home, we ignore the mile markers and run just to enjoy the scenery and collect our thoughts, when we forget we're exerting ourselves and get in the zone...that is our "runners high."

Most times, before heading out for a run I ask myself why do I run? So today, I decided to find out the true answer to why. On this day, without my ipod, and without any running partners, it was just me and the pavement. As I went along, I started to realize that throughout my life, there have been many barriers set before me which were difficult to overcome but ultimately my heart and my soul always guided me down the right path. Through running and fitness, I realized I've gained confidence.

Not only confidence in myself, but the confidence that nothing can stop me. The confidence that I will let nothing stand in my way.

Running and fitness have opened my eyes to a whole different world. The world of "me." The world where I have learned to care about myself. Not is a selfish way, but in a self-worth way. I deserve to be the best I can be, and the only way to do that is to take care of myself. If I don't, then who will? We are solely responsible for ourselves! The world where I realized that if i don't care for myself first and be happy as me, that I am unable to make anyone else surrounding me happy.

So on that specific day when I got back from my run, I looked into the mirror and what I saw was a determined confident person who will never accept defeat without putting forth a strong effort. It was at that moment that I finally realized that I was somebody special, if to no one else at least to myself. So, tomorrow, with the scent of trees in my nose, car horns flooding my ears, and the morning breeze making my eyes water, I will once again head back out to do what I do best....and that is to take care of me!

- Heather Imielinski

Illustrative Journal, by Cindy Snow

I had tried running in the past but never found my groove. I never stuck with it long enough to learn why someone enjoyed running. I always said that I would run all day playing soccer or softball but could not just run.

Two years ago, my husband watched his father's health deteriorate and saw himself on the same path. He decided to start a home workout program called P90X. He felt that if we did it together, we would be more likely to continue the program. I worked through the program as it was designed for the 90 days. He did most of the program but had difficulty with the workouts that contained a great deal of jumping so he would go to the gym on those days instead.

Three quarters of the way through he heard of a race called the Warrior Dash. He thought it would be a great way to show off how far we had come physically. The Warrior Dash is a 5k with a dozen obstacles. I was ready for the obstacles (climbing a 15 foot wall, trudging through mud up to my knees, wading through water up to my waist, crawling under barbed wire while in mud, etc.) but I needed to get myself ready for the running portion of the race.

The first time I went out running, I decided to see how long I could run without stopping. I only lasted seven minutes. I walked for a few minutes to catch my breath and ran/walked for a bit more.

Each day I got out there and pushed myself to make it further than the day before. By the time of the race, which was only about a month, I was up to about two miles. The race was tough but I did finish in the top third of my age bracket. Afterwards, I continued with the P90X program and added in the running for cardio.

Over time, I found that running gave me an inner peace. My mother was battling cancer during the same time that I learned why runners run. It was a time when it was just me and all me. I was able to work through my stress, anxiety, and fear and push myself to greater lengths than I thought possible. I would talk to my mom in my head and tell her how much I loved her and that she was going to pull through. I pushed myself when the pain came or when I felt like giving up because she couldn't give up so neither could I.

I have learned that when I am done my run that there is a sense of satisfaction and accomplishment that I feel and when I round that last corner, I give it all I've got left. Some days that's more than others. But that is life. I take one run at a time.

Two years later, I am still doing P90X, a modified version, and I am able to run for at least 35 minutes. If someone were to ask me today, I would still say, "I am not a runner but I do run."

My favorite time to run is early in the morning between 5-6am. There are few cars on the road, few people out, and it is still dark. I don't take my phone. It is just me and my pedometer. I like this time because on a clear night the stars are still out and through my run the sun is coming up.

It is the hope of a new day.

Without the cars and people running about at that time of day to distract me, I am able to focus on my breathing, the ground beneath my feet, and the beauty that surrounds me. I don't have any demands from phones, computers, texts, or emails. My biggest demand is what I put on myself to get the most out of the run.

- Cindy Snow

One Minute Respite

Engage in the following practice anytime your anxiety level is high, but your free time is short...

Take a seat in a comfortable chair and bring your attention to your midsection. Observe the expansion and contraction of your diaphragm with your breathing.

During each inhalation, think to yourself, *"I am mastering tranquility."*

During each exhalation, think to yourself, *"I am grateful for who I am."*

Repeat 15-20 times.

Feel your body unwind.

Parting Thoughts

I have spent most of my life living in the great state of New Jersey. Walking the boardwalks near the Atlantic Ocean in my youth was the highlight of the year. The tranquility of the sea under normal conditions is God's gift that feeds my soul. Eating cotton candy, custard ice cream, playing miniature golf and braving the roller coasters on the "boards" was the rite of passage that made tolerating the long cold winters seem okay.

At an early age I embraced the cold days and frigid nights and traveled into even colder temperatures in the mountains of Vermont, New Hampshire, Maine and Pennsylvania.

I have come to love the long walks by the fast running creeks, fly fishing, canoeing, and of course cross country skiing through the woods near the frozen lakes.

Being out in nature has been a way of life that afforded me a peaceful refuge simply by exploring the great outdoors. The visualizations I've written are from direct experience with the unique quality of life known to all who value and enjoy the natural landscape.

The goal is stress prevention and my suggested methods – positive visualized meditation, journey out into nature and maintain excellent physical fitness and proper nutrition.

Appendix

B vitamins: Anti Stress Supplementation

The neurotransmitters serotonin and dopamine are important in the body's response on stress. Serotonin and dopamine helps balances the mood.

Vitamin B1
Vitamin B1 or thiamine can help in reducing one's stressful feelings.

Vitamin B2
Vitamin B2 also called riboflavin can reduce the physical symptoms of stress which are commonly headache and depression.

Vitamin B3
Vitamin B3 also known as niacin functions in the make-up of the neurotransmitter, serotonin. This neurotransmitter is the one in-charge of a person's sense of tranquility.

Vitamin B5
Pantothenic acid, the name for Vitamin B5 is important in the proper functioning of the adrenal glands. This gland is the

responsible to the production of hormones which regulate stress. Moreover, vitamin B5 helps in the production of acetylcholine in the brain. This neurotransmitter manages concentration and focus.

Vitamin B9

Vitamin B9 or folic acid helps in reducing the effect homocysteine in the brain. This is according to the National Center for Health and Wellness. Homocysteine is a byproduct of some of the brain's processes and it influences how one handles stressful situations. When left unchecked, homocysteine can lead to some psychiatric disorders.

Vitamin B12

Vitamin B12 plays an important role in the proper functioning and health of the nerves. The insufficiency from vitamin B12 can lead to irritability, confusion, anxiety and stress according to the National Institutes of Health.

Since B vitamins are water-soluble, they cannot be stored in the body. Achieving the daily requirements for each of the B vitamins is the key to relieving anxiety and stress. They can be found in a lot of food sources but they also be taken as supplement to meet the RDA.

Food Sources That Help Mitigate Stress

Asparagus

This green veggie is high in folic acid, which can help stabilize your mood.

Beef

Beef contains high levels of zinc, iron, and B vitamins, which are also known to help stabilize your mood.

Milk

Milk is high in antioxidants and vitamins B2 and B12, as well as protein and calcium.

Cottage Cheese and Fruit

Cottage cheese is high in protein and calcium.

Almonds

A good source of Vitamin B2 and E, as well as magnesium and zinc, almonds are high in fat, but most of the fat is unsaturated. Like vitamin C, vitamin E has been shown to fight the free radicals associated with stress, and in particular, those free radicals that cause heart disease.

Blueberries

Very rich in antioxidants, blueberries offer a high-fiber, low-calorie fruit option that is also rich in stress-fighting vitamin C. Try them with cottage cheese or as a snack on their own.

Tuna

Tuna is high in stress-fighting vitamins B6 and B12. Tuna is also a good low-fat protein source.

Cornflakes or Crispy Rice Cereal

Cornflakes and crispy rice cereal are fortified with B vitamins and folic acid to help reduce stress. Have them for breakfast with milk.

Natural Prevention

By Maria T. Bohle, CHC, RS (Hom), ACACN

Our bodies were meant to be a perfect tool for us to go through our life, however things often go wrong and we need to know what to do to repair the problem.

Today, we pick up the phone and call our doctors, after a very brief interview most patients are given a prescription and sent on their way, they are only to return if it doesn't work. Is this really the way life should be? Get sick and go on a chemical for the rest of your life?

Yes, our bodies are a fined tuned, living breathing machine that is meant to last for the rest of our life. So, what goes wrong and why do we get sick? The famous homeopathic physician, Samuel Hahnemann felt that 85% of the people got sick due to deficient nutrition. He called it psora – the deficiency disease.

If all the nutrients that we needed were there when our body broke down we would not get sick and we would not get diseases, good nutrition means the body can repair the damage. One researcher kept a chicken heart alive for 26 years or so in a beaker of nutritional fluids, every day the heart repaired and replaced dead cells and every day he would scrape off those old dead cells. That heart apparently died at the hands of one of his graduate students when he went on vacation, I am told they were quite bored with the project by then.

Dr. Tom Smith, the author of the British Institute of Homeopathy's Clinical Nutrition Course, used to say if you are looking in the mirror at yourself and look older, your nutrition is not up to par.

So, what do we need? We need a good source of easily available nutrients. No, this does not mean you should go to your closest health food store and buy multivitamins (although some of us may need them), it means you should eat the most nutritious, natural, whole foods that you can. Some people have a slow metabolism and those people can easily be poisoned by mega vitamins. Anything we eat must be processed by our bodies. Too much of a good thing is just as bad, if not worse than not enough. For a silly example, if I am trying to cook and I do not have any salt I will need to get some salt. But if someone brought in a huge palate of 50 pound bags of salt and put them on my kitchen floor, it would be overkill, a little bit of salt is one thing, my ability to lift, lug, move and eliminate a whole stack of 50lb salt bags is easily going to overpower my energy reserves. My body is going to have to work overtime to get rid of the excess, the same thing happens inside our bodies.

There are books out there saying let food be your medicine this is the best advice, eat real food, the food God made, such as wholesome (organic if possible) vegetables, fruits, nuts and even meats are meant to be eaten by us, and they should have all the nutrients we need for optimal health. We cannot rely on prepared foods that are mass and chemically produced, fast foods that are overly processed, or artificial foods that might look and taste real but are really fancy chemicals. Read labels, if you cannot pronounce what is on the label, chances are it is not a natural food.

If you want to fortify your nutrition, there are some food that we consider miracle foods, these are foods that are almost perfect and can almost keep you alive and healthy even if you ate nothing else, it is good to eat them whenever possible: eggs (especially cage free) they are a perfect food that Tom Smith said everyone should eat at least 2 a day, avocado, sardines (they help repair DNA), coconut are some. Chorella algae, Kelp and some seaweeds, even parsley is a vitamin pill in a plant. Add brewer's yeast, leafy green vegetables are excellent. For fats, avoid most vegetable oils – olive is great, coconut oil is excellent, flaxseed and a little bit of sesame is fine and the Omega 3 fish oils are wonderful, yes even butter is good for you – If God made it, it is good in my book. Nuts are great, make sure they are fresh and watch out for nut allergies in some people. Milk if you can tolerate it is a good food, that definitely includes yogurts and fermented products that can help with beneficial populations in the colon. Fruits are great, berries are fantastic, but may have a lot of sugar calories so be aware, chose the fruit itself over the juice. Eat foods in season, yes we never had strawberries in winter, if we eat our fill during the correct season, we will not want the tasteless, vitamin deficient offseason ones. Pick your colors, yellow (Squash and Sweet potatoes are excellent), orange carrots, greens, red and purples for a color balance that also will balance your nutrition.

Watch your grains, chose the lesser known grains, wheat, corn and some other grains are genetically engineered to produce much greater yields and are not so good for us anymore. Watch the 'bread' habit which has put too much weight on most of us.

And, finally, minerals, we might just be a bit mineral deficient, Magnesium is one of the main minerals used for relaxation, Calcium is essential, if we eat right we will get plenty of calcium and magnesium from our green and leafy vegetables, but we rarely eat enough of them, Make it a priority to add green leafy vegetables to each meal, you will be happy you did.

Wait, you say, this sounds suspiciously like a very primitive diet. Yes, it is, we have eaten this way for millions of years, it has worked for our ancestors, it will work for us. How do we balance millions of years of eating primitive foods and then think we can survive and be healthy on extruded French fries, vegetable oils we never had – corn and rapeseed oils (that one is canola, but no one would buy anything called 'rape seed' so they sold us an angelic sounding name 'canola' sounds so benign doesn't it?

If our bodies are stressed, and today's society will do that very easily to all of us, we will use up certain nutrients very quickly. Vitamin C is one of them. If someone sneaks up behind you and says, "Boo" that is the end of your vitamin C says Dr. Tom Smith. So indulge yourself in real foods that contain a lot of vitamin C – so ok, maybe a supplement here can help.

Vitamin D is essential, we get that from the sun. The sun shines on our skin and eliminates cholesterols, the sun just blasts our cholesterols into Vitamin D and a good sugar called glycogen – so if your cholesterols are up – you are NOT getting enough sun! Get your bathing suit on and sunbathe, or go sit with a good book in a sunny window in shorts and a short sleeved shirt.

B vitamins are also essential, they help to relax the body, but they must be in a balance in the body, taking B vitamins individually (except B6 you can have a lot more of that one) you will cause some major B vitamin deficiencies as they all work together and will increase the need for the ones you do not have.

Brewers Yeast is an excellent, and safe source of B vitamins, that is the taste and flavor we get from fresh baked bread, I put in in my yogurt, when it tastes super delicious to me, I know I need it, when I don't want it anymore, I know my body stores are sufficient. But, I do sneak a tablespoon in my pancake mix and whenever I bake anything that easily accommodates that flavor.

My final plea, get plenty of sleep, adhere to your spiritual path and just be yourself, you cannot improve on perfection, learn to recognize the perfection in yourself.

And, if you are having a health problem, look to a gentle solution first, see a professional in that field, look at herbal medicines (nutrients and medicines in plants, easy to take and easy on the body), look at homeopathy the gentle correction, save your chemical medicine as a last resort. And finally, every time we are not true to ourselves, our body feels it, speak your truth quietly, and love one another.

I wish you radiant and good health.

Maria T. Bohle, CHC, RS (Hom), ACACN
Professional Homeopath, Herbalist & Clinical Nutritionist
Director
The British Institute of Homeopathy
(609) 927-5660

> "I go to nature to be soothed and healed, and to have my senses put in order."
>
> - John Burroughs

Acknowledgements

All of the contributors to this book value the Earth's limitless natural beauty.

Thank you to the ladies who shared their running stories with us in the illustrative journals: Shawn Acosta, Heather Imielinski, Cindy Snow and Lt. Col. Diana Brown. I so admire your discipline and perseverance but mostly your friendship! I love you all.

Barbara Snow contributed the Jersey beach photo and is my beach bum buddy. Thank you Barbie.

I will try now to thank my son, Dave, who normally deletes this part. Dave is an amazing fitness trainer who shares his skills at Tranquil Seas Retreats and with me so that I can be up to the task of running the retreats and writing the books! He tweets at @DDworkouts!

Kip Hoffman has spent a lifetime as an outdoor adventurer. He travels North America photographing the majestic images of the wilderness.

About The Author

As the owner and administrator of "Tranquil Seas" Retreats, Nora D'Ecclesis has a long history of presenting events focused on wellness and stress reduction techniques. A typical Tranquil Seas Retreat is a weekend-long group getaway to the beach or mountains, during which experts in each particular discipline treat attendees to a selection of lectures and activities that give them the knowledge to advance their lives physically, emotionally and spiritually.

Nora has compiled a variety of effective techniques and practices and illuminated them in her books, "Mastering Tranquility," "Tranquil Seas," and "Reiki Roundtable."

Nora is a graduate of Kean University, also holding a graduate degree in education, post-graduate certification as a learning specialist, and the rank of Shihan as a Usui Reiki Master. She enjoys canoeing, fishing and archery. Nora lives with her family in a suburb of Philadelphia, Pennsylvania.

For more information, visit www.noradecclesis.com or contact her by email at noradecclesis@gmail.com

NOTES

www.ingramcontent.com/pod-product-compliance
Lightning Source LLC
Chambersburg PA
CBHW071659040426
42446CB00011B/1843